THE FIRST BOOK OF SOPRANO SOLOS

compiled by Joan Frey Boytim

G. SCHIRMER, Inc.

DISTRIBUTED BY

HAL•LEONARD®
CORPORATION
7777 W. BLUEMOUND RD. P.O. BOX 13819 MILWAUKEE, WI 53213

PREFACE

Repertoire for the beginning voice student, whether teenager, college student, or adult, always poses a great challenge for the voice teacher because of the varied abilities and backgrounds the students bring to the studio. This series of books for soprano, mezzo-soprano and alto, tenor, and baritone and bass provides a comprehensive collection of songs suitable for first and second year students of any age, but is compiled with the needs of the young singer in mind.

In general, students' first experiences with songs are crucial to their further development and continued interest. Young people like to sing melodious songs with texts they can easily understand and with accompaniments that support the melodic line. As the student gains more confidence, the melodies, the texts, and the accompaniments can be more challenging. I have found that beginning students have more success with songs that are short. This enables them to overcome the problems of musical accuracy, diction, tone quality, proper technique, and interpretation without being overwhelmed by the length of the song.

Each book in this series includes English and American songs, spirituals, sacred songs, and an introduction to songs in Italian, German, French and Spanish. Many students study Spanish in the schools today, and most studio volumes do not include songs in this language; therefore, we have included two for each voice type.

Several songs in the collections have been out of print in recent years, while others have been previously available only in sheet form. Special care has been taken to avoid duplication of a great deal of general material that appears in other frequently used collections. These new volumes, with over thirty songs in each book, are intended to be another viable choice of vocal repertoire at a very affordable price for the teacher and student.

Each book contains several very easy beginning songs, with the majority of the material rated easy to moderately difficult. A few songs are quite challenging musically, but not strenuous vocally, to appeal to the student who progresses very rapidly and who comes to the studio with a great deal of musical background.

In general, the songs are short to medium in length. The ranges are very moderate, yet will extend occasionally to the top and the bottom of the typical voice. The majority of the accompaniments are not difficult, and are in keys that should not pose major problems. The variety of texts represented offers many choices for different levels of individual student interest and maturity.

In closing, I wish to thank Richard Walters at Hal Leonard Publishing for allowing me to be part of this effort to create this new series of vocal collections. We hope that these books will fill a need for teachers and students with suitable, attractive and exciting music.

Joan Frey Boytim

CONTENTS

THE BEATITUDES

Matthew 5:3-6

Albert Hay Malotte

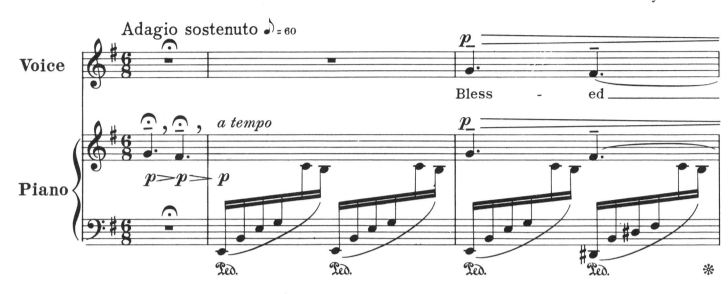

6

BEL PIACERE

Bel piacere è godere fido amor!
questo fà contento il cor.
Di bellezza non s'apprezza lo splendor
se non vien d'un fido cor.

To enjoy a devoted love
brings contentment to the heart.
If there is no faithful heart,
there is no beauty, no wisdom, and no fascination.

George Frideric Handel

Bel pia - ce - re___ è go - de - re

fi - do _ a - mor! bel pia - ce - re _

é go - de - re fi - do _ a - mor!

que - sto fà _ con - ten - to il cor, que - sto fà _ con -

mf

ten - to il cor, fà con - ten - to il cor,

que - sto fà ____ con - ten - to il cor, que - sto

fà ____ con - ten - to il cor, fà con -

ten - to il cor.

Fine

Di bel - lez - za non s'ap - prez - za___ lo splen - dor,

_p_

se non vien d'un___ fi - do cor,___d'un fi - do cor;

di bel - lez - za___ non s'ap - prez - za lo___ splen - dor,

_tr_

se non vien d'un___ fi - do cor,___d'un fi - do cor.

_mf_

D.S. al fine

BONNE NUIT
(Good Night)

Jules Massenet

Un pe - tit toit mon - te seul Au jar - din sous le til - leul,_
A lit - tle cot, scarce 'tis seen, Hides a - mid a gar - den green,

Il porte une hum - ble tou - rel - le,
It bears an hum - ble wee tow - er, Un_ oi - se - let_ dans son nid
Where a bird - ling watch - es o'er the scene

Ga_ zouille et fait sen - ti - nel - - le. Bon - ne
Twit - t'ring in its leaf - y bow - - - er: Sweet good

nuit, bon - ne nuit, bon - ne nuit!
night, sweet good night, sweet good night!

Dans la tou-relle une en-fant S'est en-dor-mie en rê-vant—
This tow-er holds, hap-py nest, A sleep-ing child, sweet-ly blest,—

A la fleur frai-che comme el-le, Le ciel la garde et re-luit
Dreams she of the flow'rs al-so sleep-ing, May Heav'n, re-flect-ed in her breast,

En son â-me jeu-ne et bel- -le. Bon-ne nuit, bon-ne
From all harm her young life be keep- -ing! Sweet good night, sweet good

nuit, bon-ne nuit!
night, sweet good night!

EL TRA LA LA Y EL PUNTEADO

Es en balde, majo mío,
Que sigas hablando,
Porque hay cosas que contesto
Yo siempre cantando.
Por mas que preguntes tant,o,
En mi no causas quebranto,
Ni yo he de salir de mi canto.

It's no use, my majo,*
For you to keep trying,
Because there are times when I answer
Always with a song.
Keep on pestering me,
You cannot upset me.
I will continue singing my song.

* majo is an untranslatable word for a dashing, handsome lover

Enrique Granados

Allegro

Es en bal - de ma - jo mi - o que si - gas ha -

blan - do, por que hay co - sas que con - tes - to yo siem - pre can - tan - do.

al Coda

Tra la la la la la la la la la la la la la la la la la.

p

Por mas que pre - gun - tes tan - to.

THE CRUCIFIXION

from The Speckled Book, 12th century
translated by Howard Mumford Jones*

Samuel Barber

*From *Romanesque Lyric*, by permission of the University of North Carolina Press.

EL MAJO DISCRETO
(My Discreet Sweetheart)

F. Periquet
translated by Olga Paul

Enrique Granados

Di - cen que mi ma - jo es
They tell me, my sweet-heart

fe - o, Es po - si - ble _ que si que lo se - a
has no looks, And in say - ing _ this, they may have rea - son,

22

EVERYWHERE I LOOK

Molly Carew

THE GREEN DOG

words and music by
Herbert Kingsley

If my dog were green

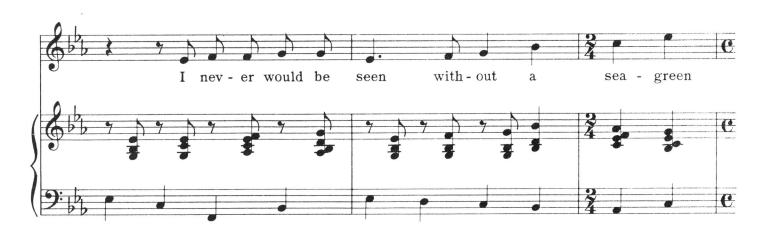

I nev - er would be seen with - out a sea - green

bon - net_____ with an e - nor - mous feath - er up -

But, a-las! no mat-ter what you've heard, The facts are con-sis-tent-ly ab-

surd, _____ For my dog is-n't green, _____

l.h. l.h. l.h.

And, what sets the mat-ter e-ven more a - gog—

_ff_

I have-n't an-y dog!

_mf_

colla voce

fff

HAVE YOU SEEN BUT A WHITE LILY GROW

Ben Johnson

Anonymous, time of James I

Have you seen but a white lil-y grow,_____ Be-

fore rude hands have touch'd it? Have you mark'd but the fall of the snow, Be-

fore the earth hath__ smucht it? Have you felt the wool of bea-vor? Or

swan's down ev-er? Or have smelt of the bud of the bri-ar? Or the

nard of the fire? Or have tast-ed the bag of the bee? O so white, O so

soft, O so sweet is she, so sweet is she; O so

white, O so soft, O so sweet, so sweet,__ so sweet is she.

HEAR MY CRY, O GOD

César Franck

God, ___ at - tend un - to my prayer; ___ From the end of the earth ___

HEFFLE CUCKOO FAIR

Rudyard Kipling

Martin Shaw

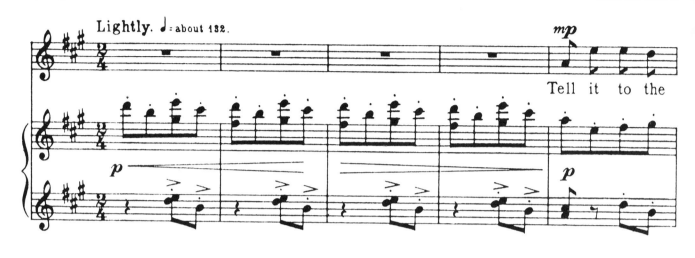

U.K. Sole Selling Agents:
WILLIAM ELKIN MUSIC SERVICES, Station Road Industrial Estate, Salhouse, Norwich NR13 6NY, England
New York: G. Schirmer Inc., Sole Agents for U.S.A.

Tell him squat and square - a! Old Wo-man! Old Wo-man! Old

Wo-man's let the Cuc-koo out At Hef-fle Cuc-koo Fair - a!

March has search'd and A-pril tried—

'Tis-n't long to May now, Not so far to Whitsun-tide, And Cuckoo's come to stay now!

THE K'E

from the Chinese, 718 B.C.

Celius Dougherty

*Pronounced **kay**

43

46

I LOVE ALL GRACEFUL THINGS

Kathleen Boland

Eric H. Thiman

* Available in Key G. Curwen Edition 71977

mong the corn, The set - ting sun, when day - light dies. The au - tumn dance of

with - er'd leaves, The snow-flakes stea - dy, gen - tle fall, The

gleam - ing slant of A - pril rain, I love them all, I love them all,

I love them all.

INTO THE NIGHT

words and music by
Clara Edwards

51

count - less wea - ry steps__ I do not heed Tho' they be

o - ver land__ or bound - less sea; I care not where the road may

lead _____ If I but come a - gain at last to thee.

Si - lent - ly in - to the night I go, In - to the

LET MY SONG FILL YOUR HEART

words and music by
Ernest Charles

56

Let my song____ fill your heart____

_ With its mel-o-dy oh so di-vine,____ That thrills me like a dream __

_ Of hap-pi-ness su - preme. ___ It's en-chant-ing, ___ it's sub-lime! ____ Let my

song _____ say the words _____ That my lips are a -

fraid to say _____ Of the yearn - ing _____ And of de - sires

burn - ing ___ To hold you and to fold you So close to my heart. _____

rall.

rall.

a tempo

MINNELIED

Felix Mendelssohn

Wie der Quell so lieb-lich klin-get, und die zar-ten Blu-men küsst, wie der Fink im Schatten sin-get, und das na-he Liebchen grüsst! Wie die Lich-ter zit-ternd schweifen, und das Gras sich grü-ner freut, wie die

Sweet-ly sounds the splashing foun-tain Where it kiss-es flow'r-y leas, Sweet the breez-es on the mountain, And the song-ster's mel-o - dies. How the flash-ing sun-beams quiv-er, And the pine - tree skyward tow'rs! Green the

LET US DANCE, LET US SING

from "Dioclesian"

Henry Purcell

LIED DER MIGNON
(Mignon's Song)

Franz Schubert

Ye who have yearned a - lone My grief can meas-ure, Ye who have yearned a - lone_ My grief can meas - ure! No friends are near and flown Are joy_ and pleas - ure; In yon-der sky I see But one_ di - rec - tion, He's far, who gave to me His _ heart's af - fec - tion. I'm

Nur wer die Sehn-sucht kennt, weiss, was_ich lei - de, nur wer die Sehn-sucht kennt, weiss, was_ich lei - de! Al - lein und ab - ge-trennt von al - ler Freu - de, seh' ich an's Fir - ma-ment nach je - ner_ Sei - te. Ach! der mich liebt und kennt, ist __ in __ der Wei - te. Es

A LITTLE CHINA FIGURE

Ethel Lindsay

Franco Leoni

Allegro con spirito

A lit - tle chi - na fig - ure On a lit - tle brack - et sat; ___ His lit - tle feet were al - ways crossed, He wore a lit - tle hat. And ev - 'ry morn - ing, fair or foul, In shine or shad - ows dim, ___ A

pret - ty lit - tle house-maid came, And soft - ly dust - ed him.____

____ She took him up so gen - tly, And with

such a charm-ing air,____ His chi - na soul was melt - ed quite And

loved her to de - spair. All day he sat and thought of her, Un-

One day, while be - ing dust - ed, In his joy he trem - bled so _____ To feel her lit - tle fin - gers, that A - las! she let him go. In vain she tried to grab him back, Fate

70

die. And on the fol-low-ing morn-ing, when The shut-ters back she

thrust,___ She spoke his lit - tle ep - i-taph: "There's one thing less to

dust. Ah!_____ there's one thing less,_____ one thing

less ___ to dust."_____

LITTLE ELEGY

Elinor Wylie*

John Duke

No bird have grace Or pow'r to sing; Or an - y-

thing _____ Be kind, or fair, And you

no - where.

LOVE HAS EYES

Charles Dibdin

Sir Henry Bishop
(1776-1855)

Allegretto moderato

Love's blind, they say,— Oh! nev-er! nay,— Can words love's grace im - part?— The fan - cy weak,— The tongue may speak,—

75

LULLABY

Christina Rossetti

Cyril Scott

THE MERMAID'S SONG

Franz Joseph Haydn

84

Come with me, and we will go

where the rocks of co - ral grow, of co - ral grow, Fol - low,

fol - low, fol - low me, Fol - low, fol - low, fol - low

me.   Come with

leggieramente

86

NIGHT IS FALLING
based on the "Serenade" from the String Quartet Op. 3, No. 5

Franz Joseph Haydn
arranged by
Pauline Viardot-Garcia

English text by Willis Wager
French and Italian texts by Louis Pomey

Night is fall-ing o-ver mead-ow, And no
La nuit mon-te, tiède et som-bre,
Già la not-te s'av-vi-ci-na, vie-ni, o

star, the flow'r of shad-ow, Shines in heav-en far a-bove. But what
toi-le, fleur de l'om-bre, Ne scin-til-le au front des cieux! Mais qu'im-
Ni-ce a-ma-to be-ne, vie-ni, o Ni-ce a-ma-to ben. Del-la

mat-ter stars in heav-en When the glimpse to me is giv-en Of the
por-tent les é-toi-les Lors-que bril-lent sous tes voi-les Les é-
pla-ci-da la-gu-na, le fresc'au-ra re-spi-ra-re, le fre-

MY JOHANN
(Norwegian Dance)

Edvard Grieg
adapted by
Alexander Aslanoff

Adele Epstein

Allegretto tranquillo e grazioso

Tra, la, la, la, la, la, la, la, la, la, When I go out to dance, my Jo-hann meets me. Oh! _____ See what he's brought!

Oh! See what he's brought! Jo-hann's brought me flow-ers, Tra, la, la, la, la, la, la, la,

Allegro

Heigh! ho! thus! so! To and fro, 'round we go!

Tra, la, la, la, la, la, la_____

Tra, la, la, la, la, la, la_____

Ah_____ To and fro, 'round we go!

Tra, la, la, la, la, la, la_____

Tra, la, la, la, la, la, la_____

accelerando

cresc. ed accelerando

97

O PEACE, THOU FAIREST CHILD OF HEAVEN

from the masque "Alfred"
by James Thomson and Davis Mallet

Thomas Arne
arranged by Guy Warrack

If the opening instrumental bars are found too long, a cut may be made from ✹ to ✦

turn   with Ease and Plea-sure,   Re -

turn   with Ease and Plea-sure.   Re -

turn,   re - turn___   with

Ease___ and Plea - - - - - - - - -

- - - - - - - - - - - - sure,

with Ease___ and Plea - sure in thy___ train.

SI MES VERS AVAIENT DES AILES!
(Were My Song With Wings Provided)

Reynaldo Hahn

105

OH, WHAT A BEAUTIFUL CITY!

African American spiritual
arranged by Edward Boatner

Oh, what a beau-ti-ful city! Twelve gates a - to de city, a-Hal- le - luh!

My Lord built a-dat city,_____ And He said it was just a-four square, And He

said He want- ed you sinners_____ To meet Him in_ a - de air, 'case He built

Twelve gates a - to de city, a-Hal - le - luh. Oh, what a beau - ti - ful city!

Oh, what a beau - ti - ful city! Oh, what a beau - ti - ful city!

Twelve gates, twelve gates, Hal - le - luh!

PIERCING EYES

Franz Joseph Haydn

light.

Those

eyes— full well do know— my heart and all— its work - ings see.———

E'er since they play'd the conq' - ror's part.

And I— no more— was free,——— and I— no more— was

ROSE SOFTLY BLOOMING
from *Azor'* and *Zemira*

Louis Spohr

Tempo I

Peace - ful - ly smil - ing, Oh, let me be,

Ossia

dy - ing, Sweet rose, sweet rose, like

Liv - ing and dy - ing, Sweet rose, like

colla parte

thee! Liv - ing and dy - ing, Sweet rose, like

thee!

dim.

WALDEINSAMKEIT
(The Quiet of the Woods)

Max Reger

I - dle, un - a - ware,   Comes____ my 3 ____
mei - ner ganz ver - gass: *kommt____ mein____*

sweet - heart,   and   steals   a - round a. lin - den tree,   And
Schatz____   und   schlei - chet sich um   mich____   und

kiss - - - - es me!
küs - - - - set mich.

WATER PARTED FROM THE SEA

from "Artaxerxes"
translated from Metastastio

Thomas Arne

Though in search of lost __ re - pose __ Through the land 'tis

free __ to roam, Still it __ mur - murs as __ it __ flows,

Pant - ing for its na - tive home.

WHEN I HAVE SUNG MY SONGS

words and music by
Ernest Charles

Just you and I. I could not share them all a-

gain— I'd rath-er die_____ With just the

thought_____ that I had loved so well, so

true,_____ That I could nev-er sing a-gain,

That I could nev-er, nev-er sing a-gain, Ex-cept___ to

you._____

The tip of the tongue the teeth and
the lips